THE FLEA MARKET BOOK

for Vendors and Shoppers

Pennsylvania & New Jersey edition

THE FLEA MARKET BOOK

for Vendors and Shoppers

Pennsylvania & New Jersey edition

∞

by Manny Luftglass

For Jon

3/27/15

Enjoy !

Gone Fishin' Enterprises
PO Box 556, Annandale, NJ 08801

4

Pictured on the cover:
Here's a shot of a food vendor's table,
given to us by the folks at Rice's Sale & Country Market.

All other photos:
From the author's own collection, from the collection
of Barbara Luftglass-Morea, and from the web sites of the
various markets that allowed us to use some of their pictures,
as well as the dog in costume at Rice's Sale and Country Market.

THE FLEA MARKET BOOK
for Vendors and Shoppers
Pennsylvania & New Jersey edition
by Manny Luftglass
© 2015 Emanuel Luftglass

Published by
Gone Fishin' Enterprises
PO Box 556, Annandale, NJ 08801

ISBN: 0986043419
ISBN: 978-0986043413

Design & Typography:
Barone Graphics & Design, Bloomsbury, NJ

PRINTED BY PUBLISHERS' GRAPHICS, CAROL STREAM, IL

Table of Contents

TOWN	MARKET	PG
Adamstown (aka Denver)	Renningers Antique Market	56
Archbald	Sugarman's Market	57
Barto	Jake's Flea Market	58
Bradford	PA/NY Indoor Flea Market	59

THE FLEA MARKET BOOK
for Vendors and Shoppers

Overview

Simply, there are lots of flea markets in this country and more and more of them seem to be appearing each year. The main purpose of this book is to tell you readers about those markets that are open at least once a week on nearly a year-round basis, weather permitting, and have been in business for at least three years.

The general plan of this book is twofold, for buyers as well as sellers. I want you who are interested in attending markets as buyers as well as sellers what you can do to make your experience as enjoyable as possible. I want you to know what you will need to do to find the markets that house many vendors of assorted merchandise so that you can do one-stop" shopping for a variety of goods that will be useful to you and not create the typical "buyer's remorse" that often occurs once a shopper comes home.

This book will list the larger markets that lie within Pennsylvania and New Jersey. Some directions will be provided to each market as well as what their basic operating conditions are, such as what entrance charge and/or parking fee is involved as well as what the operating hours are per market. If I wasn't able to provide you with exact directions for every one, for sure, each market will list their address so that you can find the way to reach them via Map Quest. I will also list the days that each market is open, including holidays.

A bluebird day at the Golden Nugget.

Buyers will be given a variety of tips to help them "shop" for the best prices. Some may call this "bargaining" but if done correctly, it can be fun for them and even for the folks they are trying to get to reduce their asking price. Chances are pretty good that 90% or more of things purchased at flea markets are sold at prices that are lower than the marked price but that is part of the fun of the day, going home with a bargain, all at the same time as pleasing the seller who otherwise might have had to take the merchandise home!

On the other hand, potential vendors will be told how to get the very best chance to achieve a successful day. Included herein will be a variety of methods they should use to obtain merchandise at the best prices as well as how to get things that would be of interest to a large group of potential buyers. Our vendors will be taught how to make their merchandise look even more appealing than it looked to the vendor themselves, such as propping the goods up on small platforms at eye level rather than having everything sitting at table height. Potential vendors will learn where to go to obtain stock at the very best prices so that they can make the most money per sale.

A few basic ideas, to tweak your learning process, would include our section on "No cash —no problem," as well as "Be back," that dreadful comment made by shoppers in a variety of ways to tell a vendor that they will come back later but nearly never actually do so.

I do hope that, by reading this book, it will add to your pleasure on the day/s that you visit a flea market, as a seller or buyer. Make it a fun day and it will become one.

Dedication

Simple enough, I dedicate this book to two groups of people, first, to the countless vendors who get up in the dark and head to the market with vehicles fully loaded with all kinds of merchandise, intent on selling everything all at the same time as hoping that they don't end up back in their driveway at the end of the day with most of the stuff they brought with them. And of course, to my second group, the buyers, who I really hope will find enough things to buy each day so that they will be encouraged to visit that market and others too in the days ahead. And who knows, after five or ten such shopping sprees, some of these very buyers will one day turn into sellers later on.

THE FLEA MARKET BOOK
for Vendors and Shoppers

Acknowledgments

Having spoken directly to as many as 100 people about this book before sitting down to write the first paragraph, I cannot really list all of them. So in order to not insult anyone who spent time with me, let me simply say a great big thank you to one and all. You know who you are and when you recognize some of the things I write in this book as something you told to me, I hope that this is enough satisfaction to you, okay?

About the Author/Publisher

I was born and raised in Brooklyn, N.Y. in 1935, and, with wife and two daughters, moved to New Jersey in 1964. I quit high school (don't you do it, kids!) and went into the insurance brokerage field as a delivery boy and wound up living the American Dream, forming my own insurance agency with my co-worker, in Somerville, N.J. in 1971.

I wrote my first "Gone Fishin' " column that same year and ultimately, created a recycling program for the borough under the name WASTE, Inc. (We Are Somerville, Together for Ecology). Divorced and remarried a few years down the road, I was appointed to head the Somerville Environmental Commission and later, was elected and reelected Mayor of the borough.

I wrote and self-published my first of 23 books (this being #24) in 1994 and now live with wife #3, Karen, in Hunterdon County, N. J. where I continue to fish and write about it, as well as publish books for other authors.

The idea for this book came from my attending many flea markets, frankly. I saw the opportunity to present a first-hand view of what goes on at these markets, from the eyes of a vendor as well as a shopper. I hope you like it.

Introduction

In order to make this book timeless in scope, I have intentionally listed markets that were in business at least three years when we went to print. Therefore, you can probably count on finding each facility listed to be open when you decide to visit it. You may find some places listed that were not open a full three years but they will certainly be the exception, not the rule, in order to help. I will identify them by saying when they opened for business.

THE FLEA MARKET BOOK
for Vendors and Shoppers

Definition of a Flea Market

D epending on which dictionary you open, there are countless definitions of a "Flea Market." In fact, I found a book about flea markets that describes those of you who are or will be buyers or sellers as FLEAS! I guess she was talking about the way that fleas flitter about, from one place to another, and I suppose that it might be easy to imagine fleas in just that manner.

But when I turned to page 532 in the 1978 edition of Webster's *New World Dictionary*, I found "flea" described, in part, as "bloodsucking parasites on mammals and birds, also as wingless insects with large legs adapted for jumping."

However, a few definitions down the page, I found something that fits better for certain when I checked out "flea market." It said it pretty well here: "An outdoor bazaar dealing mainly in cheap, secondhand goods." Of course this is only a modest condensed version because some of the markets that I have visited deal with relatively expensive antiques as well as in fresh produce, plus new merchandise and without doubt, you may also find a bald guy selling the books that he published, including this very book!

A few other descriptions of a flea market that I found would include: "A market, often outdoors, consisting of individual stalls selling old or used articles, curios and antiques, cut-rate merchandise, etc." More:

"An open-air market selling cheap and often second-hand goods." Yet another definition said: "A usually outdoor market in which old and used goods are sold." Maybe the silliest one I ran into was found under World Origin & History" and it defined flea market as: "1917, especially in reference to the Fr. marché aux puces in Paris, so-called "because there are so many second-hand articles sold of all kinds that they are believed to gather fleas." And to that, I say foo on you, 99% of the vendors who I have run across sell merchandise that is either clean or even new. But still, I smiled a soft smile to myself when I read this false description.

Funny too, is the fact that most of the larger flea markets that I will write about in this book also have substantial indoor spaces to visit, most being both air-conditioned and heated.

As you drop down further, you will find some other market descriptions, not true "Flea" markets because many also include self-explanatory "Auction" markets as well as places that contain the more normal vendor booths. Further descriptions will include "Farmer's Markets," etc.

A) New products

This one could be a little tricky because "new" isn't always thus. You could find merchandise on a table that appears unused, but often, that's not the case. A fishing lure in its original box may seem new but at

The crowd is starting to build.

times, a "used" lure in its box could be worth far more than one you buy at a store, and the older, the better. For certain, if the lure is made out of wood that really may increase its value rather than drop it. But as a general rule of thumb, if it is used, you should be able to get it for less than the original list price.

B) Used products

"Used?" Clearly, if someone has already enjoyed the use of what is in front of your eyes, you should really be able to obtain it at a good price, but here again, the older it may be, the more valuable it's worth at times. Here too, if it is, for example, a toy in its original carton, the cost to you may be higher than expected. And when it comes to toys, if it makes noise, and the market is filled with kids with their grandma's, expect to see the vendor increase its cost as soon as they see the little girl tilt her head to the side and start to plead with Grammy.

For-Profit Markets

T he following list includes most of the other non-conventional places to go shopping at.

A) Farmer's markets

A "Farmer's Market" could be just that — a locale where farmers go to sell their products. Some markets started that way and evolved into full-service ones that also sell a wide variety of other types of goods. But some such markets specialize in the sale of fruits and vegetables. Of course you may find some produce that was actually born hundreds of miles away but, hey, at times, you have to take what you get.

There are markets that began as places to bring animals to for sale — some sold via conventional methods and others selling their animals at auction. But most of the original ones evolved into flea market at which one could also buy produce, animals, etc. As an example, I attend one fairly often which has a vendor who sells live rabbits and hamsters.

B) Auction markets

Here too, some markets sell goods via the traditional flea-market tables but lots of them will also have a building or two into which customers gather to participate in those fun but noisy events with an auctioneer yelling out loud to encourage bids from folks who may very well not have a bit of interest in the item being offered. However, some bidders just get "into it" and live to bid up other people, knowing, (they think, at least), when to jump off the bidding bandwagon. This enjoyment could come to a crashing halt though when the other bidders bail out, leaving the bidder-upper with the need to actually pay for something they didn't want at all.

In the "About the Buyer" section, my son-in-law, Greg Morea, a master-shopper if there ever was one, describes his methods of dealing with the many auction markets he attends each year, as well as giving you a whole pile of hints at what to do and what not to do.

My first-born, Barbara, has provided some pictures in this section of her husband's "collections."

C) "Storage Wars"

This chapter will take readers to an extreme view of what some folks will go through in order to gather as much "product" as they can in one attempt. Of course failure often occurs but many times, the result of winning a successful "war" could produce lots of dollars.

I turned to one of my best sources of information here, "Wikipedia, the free encyclopedia," to find my material. In condensed version, here is what I found. I hope it helps you as you think about joining the army of warriors.

Storage Wars (stylized as STORAGE WAR$) began as a reality television series on the A&E Network, starting in December 2010.

Several different series have appeared and chances are that more will follow. First came shows about "wars" in California, next came Texas and later on, shows about New York.

In fact, some shows can actually be seen by viewers in lots of other countries like Singapore, Canada, the United Kingdom, Norway, Germany, and elsewhere.

The basic idea for the show began in California, and to quote from Wikipedia, "When rent is not paid on a storage locker for three months in California, the contents can be sold by an auctioneer as a single lot of items in the form of a cash-only auction. Prospective bidders purchase the contents based on only a five-minute inspection of what they can see from the door when it is open."

The show got to be so popular that "its second season premiere attracted 5.1 million total viewers, making it the most-watched program in A&E's history to that point."

Now don't you go and get an idea to join the bidders in this venture, please. I just wanted to give you a view of what extent some folks go to to gather material for sale.

D) "American Pickers"

The idea for this section came while I was reading, believe it or not, the "Editor's Log," by Chris Lido in the 7/10/14 issue of the *Fisherman Magazine*!

Chris talked about the TV show and that made me think that it might be a good idea for me to write about it in this book for you.

So, once again, I went to Wikipedia for more details to share with you if you really, really want to think about dropping most of the things you do now and join in with the extreme shoppers who are featured on this new television reality show.

The show began on the History channel in 2010 and in it, to quote once more from Wikipedia, "The show follows antique and collectible pickers Mike Wolfe and Frank Fritz as well as their friend Crazy Al as they travel primarily around the United States," buying ("picking") various items either for resale, for clients, or occasionally their own personal collections. Season 4 began, in part, quoting Mike and Frank, "We're looking for amazing things buried in people's garages and barns. What most people see as junk, we see as dollar signs. We'll buy "anything" we think we can make a buck on. Each item we pick has a history all its own and the people we meet? Well, they're a breed all their own."

Here again, let me warn you that this really, really may not be something you want to do!

THE FLEA MARKET BOOK
for Vendors and Shoppers

Not-for-Profit
Markets

This chapter applies to the types of markets that are, as a general rule of thumb, open on an on-demand basis, periodically, and maybe for only a day or two yearly.

A) Charitable markets (Religious, library, etc.)

Open your local free newspaper and you will see a load of listings of markets that will be run by the neighborhood library as a fund-raiser, ditto your nearby church, synagogue or mosque. The libraries may simply be trying to offload old books but when taken to a higher level, they too may rent space for tables to area residents to sell their unwanted property at.

As an aside, if you intend to be a vendor of new books at one of the library markets, try real hard to get a commitment from the library that either no used books will be sold thereat or at least not more than one vendor will be allowed to do so.

B) Club markets

Hardly a non-profit club exists that doesn't always need more money. They need it to help with their charitable work and the more money they can raise from dues, etc., the better the assistance they can provide to area poor.

When dues won't cover their wishes, most Lions, Kiwanis, Girl and Boy Scout Troops and the like will hold a fund-raiser in the form of a market. Members are encouraged to bring their unwanted but usable items to the market the evening before so that the folks selling the goods can examine them and attempt to establish prices for every item.

More often than not, half of the goods on display will be purchased by other club members but I guess you could call that a form of recycling. But without doubt, these club markets often bring in big bucks to the club treasuries to assist them in their charitable functions.

C) Garage sale markets (Individual or multi-family)

Garage sales are held every weekend of the year and those trying to sell their goods have many motives. Some may simply be trying to unload a garage full of old clothing, toys, and games. But many are folks who were "Collectors" who, for one reason or another (the reason could be caused by the demands of one's "better half") but whatever the reason, garage sales are great places to attend to buy things at low cost.

The local newspaper ad that was placed by the homeowners holding the sale might say something like "STARTS at 9:00 a. m., and no one can buy anything before that time," but still, cars will pull up in the dark and folks will try to pick their way through what's on display to be able to decide early on what they want to buy.

The more sophisticated garage sales occur in partnership with one or more neighbors. After all, the more merchandise, the more buyers right? Some neighborhoods even do block-wide sales and others; especially in condo communities, do huge events at which every resident is allowed to sell their property to anyone wishing to buy it.

It is at such events that the high-level vendors often load their pickup trucks with tons of goods so that they can bring them to the nearby flea market and try to score big profits.

D) More markets

For certain, lots of folks get together to offer things for sale and some such sites are called "Yard Sales," "Tag Sales," and Rummage Sales." Each is kind of a variation on the other but still; let's talk briefly about them now.

1) A *yard sale* is really just that, a sale that occurs in someone's front or side yard. This could be because the owners' garage is full or maybe because they don't have a garage or it could also be a site

which has a garage sale going on with so much spillover that it changes into a yard sale! Same deal, different name.

2) A *tag sale* brings something else into play, the elimination of guess work. Some shoppers hate to ask the seller what they want for their goods, it gets embarrassing when they are ready to offer $5 for something that the seller wants $50 for. To eliminate some of this confusion the seller will often attach a small paper tag with string to the item with its asking price clearly marked on the tag. That doesn't mean that this is what the buyer will pay but it least sets an example of what the seller thinks the item is worth.

I went online at Google and found yet more about a tag sale than I thought possible. For example, the basic description of a tag sale said: A sale of second-hand items: an estate or moving sale where items are tagged/priced and displayed in a house. Simple enough.

3) A *rummage sale* could best be described as a place to go to in order to find the junkiest of junk but still, some items that you yourself may really have an interest in. Expect to get your best bargains at these places. Expect to get your hands kind of dirty here also.

E) Estate sales

Clearly, this need not specifically involve the death of someone, but many times, after folks die, their relatives pick through everything and what is left is either sold or sent to the junk yard. Such advertised sales often produce bargains galore and here too is where vendor-wannabes come to gather stock for them to sell at a later date.

Contribution from
Expert Buyer Greg Morea

G reg is my son-in-law, an engineer with General Dynamics in Ct., and a graduate of Columbia University. He is a world-class shopper, attending dozens of events yearly and has already filled up his garage, basement, and four storage sheds with the results of his shopping efforts. He will tell readers how to look for the top bargains.

Find the Mets cap!

Tips From an Obsessive Fan
of Flea Markets, Auctions and Yard Sales

As the owner of four full sheds on my property, a stuffed basement, and an overloaded garage, I feel as if I've learned a few critical lessons about purchasing treasures from flea markets and their closely related cousins, yard sales and auctions. Allow me to pass a few on to you.

First and foremost, you need to have a patient and understanding partner. My beloved wife of 30 plus years is assured a prominent place in eternal glory for all of the times I've come home with a truckload of treasures saying "sure I'll find a place for them." Both Barbara and I know that I am lying through my teeth with such words, and the items will land on her prized 1995 Mustang until I figure out where to stash them. There is direct correlation between Barbara's anger level and the speed with which I find new places to put items.

Next, realize that when you attend any of the big three gathering events (flea market, yard sale, auction), your main objective should be to have FUN. Just as beauty is in the eye of the beholder, fun at a flea market is a matter of individual taste. In general, though, if you find yourself cursing, in handcuffs, or in divorce court after spending the day at one, then perhaps you should find an alternative way of having fun.

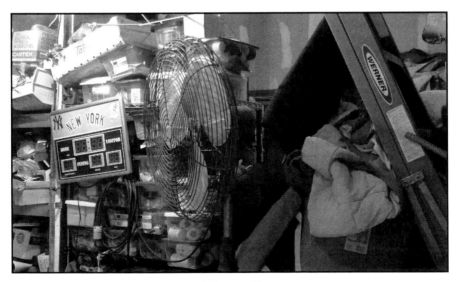

Time out!

A close corollary to having fun is to be NICE. I've yet to meet any seller who will respond favorably to a pushy, brash, or otherwise rude buyer. This is especially true when it comes to bargaining! It is never inappropriate to ask if a price is flexible or to offer a lower price for an item, as long as it's done politely. If the seller says the price is firm, then the price is firm, and you need to decide if you are willing to pay the asking price. On the other hand, if the seller is willing to negotiate, you need to keep your offer reasonable. Offering $5 for an item that you and the seller know *cost* $500 will most likely not lead to an eventual purchase. As a general rule, start your negotiating at one half of the asking price and expect to pay two thirds or so.

Notice that in the paragraph above, I've emphasized the word "cost." One of the biggest mistakes sellers make is to say what an item is *worth* when negotiating. "Worth" is decided by the buyer, not the seller, and it is very different from "cost." If someone is trying to sell me a roll of wire for $100, but I am not willing to pay more than $50 for it, then it is worth $50 to me. I don't care that you paid $200 for the wire, or that it has $125 in scrap copper in it; it is only worth $50 to me. Note also what I said above about not caring what you paid for the wire. It is a big turn-off to me for someone to say "I paid $50 for that electric drill so it is a steal at $40." OK, so you paid $50 for it, used it 3000 times, dropped it in paint, frayed the cord, and left it submerged in your boat's bilge for a month. Not a steal to me!

It is also important to know the difference between "need" and "want." Looking for truly needed items, those necessary for the sustainment of life or protection of property, is seldom (OK, never) the reason I go to a flea market, auction, or yard sale. I go to have fun, which for me means finding a treasure that I couldn't possibly live without. The phrase I just used, "couldn't live without," is flexible to me but absolutely rigid to my wife. In her eyes, "needing to live" consists of air, some foods, and everything I've already collected and stored. Since anything I might now find does not fit into the above-listed three, anything I find is a "want." Secretly, I know Barbara is completely right here, but I keep trying to convince her otherwise. My advice here is to admit that most items found are "wants," not "needs," and hope for understanding from your partner.

Finally, let me offer you some examples of what not to say/do while attending a flea market, auction, or yard sale:

- At any of the above, do not walk off with an item after finding a stash of old coins hidden in the item without talking to the seller; you need to sleep with yourself at night.
- At a yard sale, if you must be an early bird, or worse, a knocker (show up the day before a sale), ASK if it is OK to look around; if the answer is no, DON'T.
- At an auction, don't say to the winning bidder, "gee, I really wanted that item," especially if you sound snarky; if you wanted it that much, you should have bid more — that's what an auction is.
- At any event that is being held for charity, don't negotiate heavily; a simple "is this price flexible?" is all that should be said; if you receive a counter-offer, take it.
- Lastly, at any event that your partner is attending with you, if you get an emphatic NO about an item, listen; the fights which will follow if you don't are not worth it in the end.

On the last point, of course, this is advice I do not myself follow, which is why I say that my wife is a "patient and understanding partner." If she weren't, I'd be in divorce court, and her father would not be publishing this in his book!

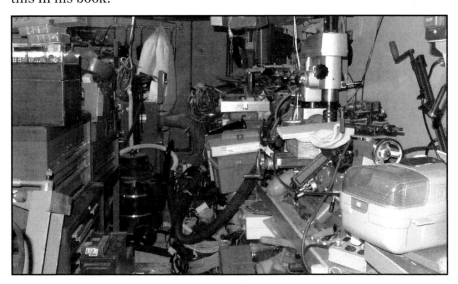

Part of a collection.

Contribution from the Eyes of a "Gatherer" (Don Luster)

I reached Don after seeing one his advertisements in our local free magazine, "The Treasure Hunt," which lists just about everything that folks want to buy or sell. We'll talk later on about this way to shop and sell.

Don can be reached at his place in Glen Gardner, N. J. and his telephone number is 908-537-4644.

Don is an independent business man who is pretty unique. He is proud to say that he is "All-American," and only deals with American-made products when he sells things. And sell he does, but first, he gathers! Don offers his services as a "clean-out" guy, saying that he will clean out your attic, basement, garage, etc., for a fee. At times, if he finds a room full of loot, he may even pay the homeowners for some of the things he picks up but many are simply too glad to get their "junk" removed to think about money coming in. Don did tell me though that the "market" went down in 2000 and gathering isn't as profitable as it used to be.

His dad started doing this in 1966 and he has been in the business all of his life. Owner of four different trucks, he uses whichever is needed in order to take care of the job, depending on how big or small it may be.

Important here is the need for me to tell you that you cannot simply buy a truck, run an ad; and then watch the money pour in. For example,

Don is licensed to do what he does, has a business license, a D. E. P. permit and a license to dump refuse. His property is zoned B2 Commercial so don't think about doing this out of your home.

Insurance is a separate need, of course, since every vehicle in New Jersey must carry liability insurance. As a former business insurance agent, I suggest that you carry at least $1,000,000 of liability insurance if you want to undertake this venture. With help from my former partner, Morgan McLachlan, I will write later on about what other kinds of insurance someone may want to carry if they want to become a flea market vendor. This could surprise some vendors!

Don brings much of the better merchandise that he picks up to three different flea markets and sells a good volume of it at these sites. They are The Island Park Flea Market in Easton, Pa., The Five Acres Flea Market in White Township, N. J., and the Golden Nugget Flea Market south of Lambertville, N. J. Five Acres rents space onto which vendors provide their own tables. The two others provide the vendor with tables as part of their rental fee.

When you get to the chapter about the actual markets in Pa. and N. J., you will see more details therein about these three.

Contribution from the Eyes of Two Auctioneers, Michael Stasak and Laurel Fox

Mike and Laurel are not your typical seller or buyer. But what they provide herein should prove to be valuable to both groups for whom this book was intended. They are auctioneers and much of what they are selling at these events can and often do prove to be very valuable to sellers so I asked them to assist and in spite of the fact that they were going to hold a huge auction in a few days, they still managed to put this information into print for me to share with you all. They can be reached at 908-763-3171 and by e-mail at justuff@enter.net.

So if you would like to have them hold an auction for you, or maybe if you want to go somewhere that you can find tons of things to sell at a flea market, by all means, try them! And now for their useful addition to our book:

Digger's delight!

As you stroll down the aisles of the antique and flea markets, do you ever wonder where all that unique merchandise came from? Mostly likely it came from one of two places: estate tag sales or auctions. Estate tag sales are basically a glorified garage sale held inside the home. The prices are set ahead of time with built-in flexibility in order to sell the goods.

When you're in the antique/liquidation business, you're bound to come across some pretty unique stuff. Attics, basements, barns and closets are my first targets when I enter a home. I love the houses that haven't been touched in years and boxes line the walls of rooms with treasures that have been packed away for 60+ years. Combing through the boxes and finding trains and toys from the 1920s and '30s that were once cherished by the young boy who is now in his '80s and living in a long-term care facility are just a few of my favorite finds. His mother's jewelry, early bake ware, clothing, Christmas ornaments and yearbooks are also favorites. You don't need to have a large home and a lot of things, but you need to have the "right" things. My first gut feeling in homes such as these is having a "digger's delight" sale. These types of sales are usually one day and last about six hours. The items are very saleable, but the quality doesn't constitute having an on-site auction. I encourage the dealers, collectors and neighbors to come sift through the items and make piles of their treasures. My goal is to empty the house, make money for the client and clear the house of the debris. The dealer's objective is to get the most for the least, have a blast finding the items, trying to decipher what the item actually was used for and determining how much of a profit is in it for them. I've found Fridays to be "dealer days" as it provides the dealer the opportunity to buy during the week and the chance to pawn it on the weekends at the markets.

Box lots are a HUGE hit at our on-site auctions. We've learned over the years there's an art to making a good box lot. Staged properly, such box lots have fetched a few hundred dollars each. It's a win-win for both me and the seller wherein it saves a lot of time and conserves my voice while it also is cost effective to the seller by saving a lot of money on hourly labor fees associated with an auction. The work associated with either one of these sales is hard, but yet very rewarding! I consider myself fortunate being able to work for myself at a job I just love!

Laurel Fox and Michael Stasak
Michael Stasak Auction and Appraisal Service

∞

Things to Know for Vendors

A) How to deal with the devil "be back" matter

Don't know what that means? There are two answers to this question: A) you have never been to a flea market or B) you also have never been to a flea market.

You see, of the countless folks who go shopping at a market there are a variety of them that really don't know how to say NO! to a vendor so they select from a list of ways to avoid getting yelled at. Top on that list is to lie, or at least, kinda lie. When they examine or at least glance at some merchandise the vendor gets all juiced up, expecting to make a sale. Trying as hard as he may, he cannot close the deal but in order to let him down gently, the shopper says something like "be back," or maybe "see ya' later" or how about "I just got here," or who knows how many varieties of that exclamation.

I've compared notes with quite a few other vendors on this point and the overwhelming majority of sellers feel that something in the neighborhood of 99% of "be backs" never do come back.

One way to deal with a "be back" is to gently push the sale harder, telling the gal who is about to turn on her heels and continue on her way down the aisle, that, "if you buy now, I'll give you another $X off the price." Maybe something like "tell me how much you want to pay?"

or how about "I'll throw in a second item of similar list price at half-off if you decide to buy right now."

Quite a few people simply don't want to drag a purchase around from table to table and that may be why they legitimately say that they will be back and many really do intend to come back. But folks, very, very few actually do. They get all caught up in the routine and simply forget where they wanted to return to and the bigger the market, the more likely this will take place. However, you can take care of this by simply offering to hold onto the merchandise in your vehicle after they pay for it and before heading home, the buyer can go to your table and gather their purchases. The bigger the item, an antique for example, the more logical this solution is, right?

B) No cash — no problem

Nearly all of the bigger markets have ATMs at which a buyer can take some money out and in such instances, the excuse no longer is valid. But some market machines may be out of service and others still could be too small to have one on hand. Here too, a buyer may not want to get their purchase money that way because of the charge they may incur.

1) *Cash*. Way above all, is the 99% favorite way to buy and 99% plus of vendors also want to sell for cash. Forgetting the devil "sales tax," to be dealt with a little later, cash is clearly the top game in town. But what if your customer's eyes got in the way of her brain and she spent her whole stash half-way down the aisles and she really, really wants to buy that thing that is staring up at her, pleading to go back home with her.

2) *Check*. Well, as noted above, "no cash" can be no problem, if your merchandise wasn't too costly to you to begin with and if you are good at sizing your prospect up. Some of the more innocent faces, of course, hide the fact that a crook is really facing you. So if they offer a check and look okay, ask to see their picture on their driver's license and write its number down.

But I really like to think that nearly everyone is honest and when the prospect tells me that they have run out of cash, etc. and don't have their check book with them, I stare them straight in the face and come back quickly with a variation of this thought: "take it home and send me a check, I trust people and really doubt that you won't pay me." I have done this 100 or more times over the years and honestly, never once was I cheated, not a single time. Again, if you laid out $100 for what you want to sell for $200, the risk of losing the "c-note" may be too great but if you paid $5 and expect $10, why not, right?

In my own case, if I am offering you a new book that lists at $13.95 for $10 and you don't have the dough, since virtually all of my books have long since gone into the "black," if and when you pay me the $10; that is found money. So if you don't pay, I lost nothing. The same thing could apply if you are trying to sell stuff that was in your attic or basement or the back of your recently passed away grand-something or another, so what, right? You didn't pay anything for it to begin with.

In these instances, and folks, please read carefully now, the system that produces payment for me 100% of the time is simple: make sure to have a supply of business cards on your table! You can use them to produce business later but in this case, it eliminates the chance of your buyer forgetting to send you a check. You may even want to have some envelopes on your table with your return address imprinted on them. Not anything I have done but, hey, why not also put a postage stamp on the envelope? It would have to be a dummy or a crook who wouldn't send you your money.

The closest I ever came to not being paid was when I was attending a fishermen's flea market in Parsippany, N. J., and a guy walked up to my table and picked up one of my books and handed me cash for it and then handed me more cash. He told me that the prior year he took a book home and promised to mail a check the next week and simply forgot about it. This time, he felt so guilty that he bought another one and paid me for the first and second ones, nice, huh?

3) *Credit card.* Few vendors that I have run across are geared up to accept credit cards but if you are very serious about trying to make money while selling at flea markets, you may want to do the paperwork necessary to be able to take credit card payments. I do suggest that you at least look into it. While a fee may be deducted by

the credit card company, you will be paid darn near immediately with the money being deposited into your checking account. Think about it at least.

4) *PayPal.* This system is "an international e-commerce business allowing payments and money transfers to be made through the Internet." Owned by eBay, this is used by lots of businesses to pay some bills and if you want to try to sell a case-load of goods to a business and that business understands PayPal, you could really hit a home run this way if you are prepared for it. I only recently got caught up to the current generation and started accepting payments via PayPal. Frankly, I've only done it a few times but at least a few sales took place this way that probably never would have occurred otherwise. Here too, check it out.

Things to Know
for Buyers

S tart off with a game plan because if you didn't do so, you could return home with a gigantic headache, a car full of who-knows-what, and an empty wallet. But if you establish a budget and try to stick to it, and decide in advance how much money to set aside for "necessary" buys as well as for "impulse" ones, you could have a really great day.

Try to know the lay of the land. Some of the bigger markets have a floor-plan of their premises built into their web sites. This could really help. If you don't know what's there to see, you may really miss an attraction or three. Some markets sprawl over lots of acres with a building or two between them and with a floor plan, you will have a good chance at covering everything you would want to check out.

If the weather is questionable but you go anyway; walk to the furthest point away from your parked car and start to weave your way back. Even if you carry an umbrella, you would rather stay completely dry and this gives you a good shot at it. Some markets aren't open in bad weather but others are so here, you may want to call ahead to be certain that they are open.

Many markets have covered sections, not full buildings but still, a place where vendors can offer their wares and you can check them out without getting wet. They are generally called "Pavilions," if the weather is bad but the market is open, you may want to head to these spots and forsake getting a soaking. But if you can stand the rain, some of your best "deals" can be wrangled from vendors who are so unhappy that they will nearly give you the stuff in order to put some of your cash in their pockets.

Again, if the place is open and it's winter-time and some of that bad white stuff is falling, head to the open enclosed buildings. Most of the merchants who sell from them will be on hand and very happy to take your money because they know that a very modest turnout of customers is what they have to expect. Here too, bargains are accomplished often. Many of these buildings sell the same type of goods that are sold from the open tables outside but you will generally find some food to buy as well, if only "comfort" food. Hey, you were uncomfortable while walking so it's only fair to get comfortable by eating a hot dog, pretzel, etc., right?

Return to a friendly face. If you've been to a market and find a vendor who seems really nice, and you buy something from her and are pleased when you get home, next time, head right to that vendor's table. Chances are that who pleased you once will do so again. Return buyers are the ones that make a vendor's day.

Caveat Emptor (Let the Buyer Beware)

In a moment, I'll go into some of the reasons a seller has to be on guard. For now though, let's start with you who carry the cash, those who make a market "work," the shopper.

Without doubt, number one on the list of what to watch out for is phony merchandise. So you who could be called an "Emptor," a buyer, look and listen. The really honest vendors will warn you in advance themselves! If the painting you have picked up is signed, the vendor should tell you if it is an original autograph or a copy of same. This is the time to go to a vendor who you have purchased from before but if it's your first time on the trail, some times your gut can warn you that this guy really, really looks shady.

If an old book is "author-signed," was it really so? Trust again, is what you need to rely on but looking at the autograph may reveal that is doesn't look like an original ink signature.

And, is that dark, dirty and rusty tin can really, really an "antique? Or did someone sit outside and beat it up to make it look far older than it actually was? The same thought applies in connection with items made out of wood. Ten years old or 100? I'm sorry about this, you folks who want to start off as a vendor without any real background in the field, because my warning to buyers is to really be careful about buying an "antique" from a vendor who you don't know to be someone who really is legitimate. Hey, but if you like it, that may be all you need to be satisfied so decide by yourself on this.

Maybe the worst problem you may enCOUNTER is, forgive the pun, COUNTERfeit stuff. Knock-offs are often found at flea markets and leather goods as well as clothing are way up at the top of the list. Ditto jewelry. If they offer it at five dollars do you really think that it is a Rolex? It may be a roll-ex but not the expensive watch. This also applies to purses, of course, one of the best culprits on the trail. If it looks like real leather and feels like real leather and is marked at ten bucks and the vendor says that it is so cheap because she just closed her store after 25 years in business and is just anxious to offload everything in order to get cash for food supplies, maybe, but maybe not, right?

The more honest merchants will actually point out flaws to you, some that you might not have found by yourself. I've seen table-neighbor Al tell a prospective buyer who is examining an old item that there is a crack on the side. Or maybe that he thinks that the piece of art may have been a reproduction rather than an original. On the other hand, to assist a shopper, Al would point out the number where barely visible, the "third of twenty copies," for example. He would also show a buyer the name of the company that made the item and often, what year it was made. These add to the value and of course, such information helps him sell and aides in convincing a buyer to buy.

Watch out for short-changing sellers. Many such acts are simply an error but there may be a few bad apples in the barrel who notice that your kid is a pain in the tail and you are anxious to move on down the lane to see other tables. So simply, when you hand the money over and get change, count it, twice, to be sure you got what you should have received. Ten tables later, as you reach into your purchase to take out a twenty to pay for something and realize it's a ten-spot that the last guy gave you, it is way, too late to go back and complain. The error may really have been an honest mistake but not many vendors will accept blame and reimburse the buyer.

∞

Caveat Venditor
(Let the Seller Beware)

A) Extra hands

Store owners are generally well equipped to deal with this problem but table vendors may not have enough experience to know what to do. Picture this: You are alone behind your table and your merchandise is spread out over its twelve foot wide surface. You may even have more space than that. Some markets allow you to have two tables and some ground space for bulk items.

So it's a rare day in the summer with bright shiny skies and everyone and their mother has come to the market to buy. Wow, right? This is when the stealers shine. You are visited by a man and his wife and two kids and each adult picks something up to examine it for possible purchase. And each has a question to ask. And each kid sees something too and picks it up. Honestly or otherwise, many an item is placed in the child's pocket, or maybe dad's pocket or mom's purse, and you are so busy that you don't ever see it occur.

So, if you see more than two hands approach your table, be on guard for what could occur. Rarely if ever is this a problem but it really does take place. Your head has to be on a rotating platform so that you can see a 180 degree arc but a trained merchant often will be able to spot a thief.

Sure, dad may not even know that junior took that water pistol but when they get home, he really doesn't have it in him to go back to the market and return the unpaid for goods.

B) Funny money

Counterfeit money is a problem that occurs every now and then too. If you are at a market to sell goods that carry a high price, you may really want to get one of those little devices that you run across a $100 bill to verify its accuracy. You could really get ripped off otherwise so for sure, let the seller beware.

C) Rubber checks

It's never happened to me, but for sure, you could get ripped off by someone trying to pass a useless check to you. So, as noted earlier, if you accept a check at your table, at least ask to see their driver's license as well as a photo I. D.

D) Credit cards

Here again, if you accept a credit card for purchase, check and double check to be sure that person is who gave you the card and also write down their driver's license number after seeing a photo ID. Not commonly done but it does occur. So here too, Caveat Venditor!

Sales Tax

T his topic is hardly ever considered at flea markets but still, one will need to know what the laws are regarding who has to collect and who has to pay sales taxes and on what goods.

A) Pennsylvania

I typed in "Pennsylvania Sales Tax Law" at Google, one of my favorite sources of information, to be able to share details with you about this. And to quote: "A sales tax is a state tax collected by a merchant on the sale price of a product. The tax is for a certain percent of the product's cost. Forty-five of the fifty states use a sales tax as a means of collecting revenue and Pennsylvania is one of them. A merchant in Pennsylvania is required to collect and pay the sales tax on taxable purchases." Of course some products aren't taxable but others are for sure and not all vendors collect and pay these taxes. A flea market vendor can wind up losing a sale if they tell a buyer they have to pay sales tax at such a market so most who do pay the state simply lay it out of their pocket, considering it a cost of doing business. Just close your eyes now and think about how many times a vendor has asked you to pay sales tax at one of these markets — few, if any, right? But still, it is the law. In fact, when I go to a market I always carry a copy of my own New Jersey Business Registration Certificate with me, including my New Jersey Sales and

Use tax certificate. No, I've never been asked to display it but still, it is a good idea to have it on hand.

Vendors are required to apply for a license from the Department of Revenue. Not all products are subject to the sales tax but you had better have a list of what is and what isn't to be sure. Whenever you may be in doubt, my suggestion is to ask your accountant. And if you prepare your own tax return, you may want to call your local tax office in the town you reside to check this out further.

You are supposed to collect sales tax at the point of sale in the Keystone State. A very specific method is described in the law but the bottom line is that you are required to collect the tax and pay it to the state within a given period of time in order to avoid a fine.

Of course religious, non-profit and volunteer fire companies are not required to collect or pay sales tax but they must apply to the state for a tax-exempt certificate.

Some items such as everyday clothing, pre-packaged foods, medicines and others are not subject to a state sales tax but here you need to be sure what is and what isn't.

A common misconception is that things purchased from a catalog, over the Internet, in another state or over the telephone and other instances aren't subject to sales tax. Well, maybe not, but still the buyer has to pay a "use tax" to the state on such purchases. Whether folks do that is another item completely but still, a 6% tax is required in Pennsylvania and even more if you live in Allegheny or Philadelphia County!

B) New Jersey

Same deal, more or less, is required in the Garden State. A document I obtained on line describes state law, in part, this way: "Sales and Use Tax applies to receipts from retail sale, rental, or use of tangible personal property or digital property," massages, restaurant meals,

prepared food, hotel room rental, even parking charges. Again though, is this done each and every time? Hey, it's not for me to judge, it is, however, something that I felt I was obliged to share with you.

The document I described above in the Pennsylvania section of sales tax, my Business Registration Application, aka Form NJ-REG, is the system that New Jersey requires folks to have and even to display at each place of business, for example, at your table!

This section shouldn't be taken as a lecture or as a pain in the tail trying to tell you what to do and why you have to do it. Please just look at it as simply my feeling that I was obliged to at least talk to you a little about the law in both states.

This being a two-state book, I'll leave out any further details regarding which other states may have the same, different, or no sales tax laws. But I hope that I will soon be able to bring you a separate book about the markets in New York and thereafter, those in New England and maybe one about the many sites in Florida.

New Hope Flea Market sign. See page 69 for details.

List of Markets

This chapter lists 15 markets in Pennsylvania and 10 in New Jersey, alphabetically by town. To find the markets by name, please check the table of contents.

Pennsylvania

City	Adamstown (also called Denver)
Name of Market	Renningers Antique Market
Address	2500 N. Reading Rd., Denver (Adamstown), PA 17517
Phone	717-336-2177
Email	N/A
When Market Began	50+ years ago
Months of Operation	Year-round (This is an antique market only!)
Days Open	Sundays, plus special events
Hours of Operation	8 am to 4 pm inside, 4 am to 3 pm outside plus pavillion
Total Size/Acreage	40 acres
Number of Outdoor Vendor Spaces	300
Space Size	10' x 12' pavilion, 15' x 20' outside
Tables Provided	Yes
Indoor Buildings and Total Size	60,000 sq. ft.
Air-Conditioned and/or Heated	Yes
Charge to Vendors	$5 on up, depending on site and size
Customer Parking Lot	Fits hundreds of cars — and free
Food Services	Yes, several vendors
Toilet Facilities	Yes, two separate restroom buildings
ATMs	Yes

City	Archbald
Name of Market	Sugarman's Market
Address	600 Scranton Carbondale Highway, Archbald, PA 18403
Phone	570-876-4098
Email	N/A
When Market Began	2000
Months of Operation	Year-round
Days Open	Saturdays and Sundays plus holidays
Hours of Operation	9 am to 5 pm
Total Size/Acreage	80,000 Square Feet
Number of Outdoor Vendor Spaces	100+
Space Size	Varies
Tables Provided	No, bring your own
Indoor Buildings and Total Size	Quite sizeable
Air-Conditioned and/or Heated	Yes
Charge to Vendors	Varies, from $200 monthly on up
Customer Parking Lot	200+ cars and free
Food Services	At times
Toilet Facilities	Three each for men and women
ATMs	Yes

City	Barto
Name of Market	Jake's Flea Market
Address	1380 Route 100, Barto, PA 19504
Phone	610-845-7091
Email	info@jakesfleamarket.com
When Market Began	1980
Months of Operation	April to Christmas
Days Open	Saturdays and Sundays plus Labor Day
Hours of Operation	8 am until end
Total Size/Acreage	Big!
Number of Outdoor Vendor Spaces	Lots!
Space Size	16' x 25' including your vehicle
Tables Provided	Yes, eight feet long
Indoor Buildings and Total Size	Sorry, couldn't get an answer
Air-Conditioned and/or Heated	Sorry, couldn't get an answer
Charge to Vendors	$10 each table or two for $18 outside, same each day
Customer Parking Lot	Ample and free
Food Services	No vendor may sell any food, drink, or tobacco
Toilet Facilities	Yes, newly built in 2006
ATMs	No
NOTE: No pets or alcohol allowed	

City	Bradford
Name of Market	PA/NY Indoor Flea Market
Address	200 West Washington Street, Bradford, PA 16701
Phone	814-791-9121
Email	rick@panygarage.com
When Market Began	Just opened in 2013, call first!
Months of Operation	Year-round, it's indoors!
Days Open	Saturdays and Sundays including some holidays
Hours of Operation	9 am–4 pm Saturdays, 11 am–5 pm Sundays
Total Size/Acreage	30,000 sq. ft. inside and outside spaces too
Number of Outdoor Vendor Spaces	Ample
Space Size	N/A
Tables Provided	No, bring your own inside and outside
Indoor Buildings and Total Size	30,000 sq. ft.
Air-Conditioned and/or Heated	Both
Charge to Vendors	$25/weekend indoors, $10/weekend outdoors
Customer Parking Lot	100 cars, free
Food Services	Yes! Restaurant seats up to 40 people!
Toilet Facilities	Yes, indoors
ATMs	Yes

City	Dover
Name of Market	Newberrytown Peddlers Market
Address	700 York Road, Dover, PA 17315
Phone	717-932-4264
Email	peddlersmkt@aol.com
When Market Began	A while back!
Months of Operation	Year-round including some special events
Days Open	*Flea market:* Saturdays and Sundays 8 am–3 pm; *Farmer's market:* Saturdays 8 am–4 pm
Hours of Operation	See above, and they hold some auctions too!
Total Size/Acreage	Ample acreage
Number of Outdoor Vendor Spaces	Lots of them
Space Size	12' x 20'
Tables Provided	No, bring your own
Indoor Buildings and Total Size	Yes, and covered pavilions are on hand
Air-Conditioned and/or Heated	N/A
Charge to Vendors	$10 each space, every day
Customer Parking Lot	Ample and free!
Food Services	Yes
Toilet Facilities	Yes
ATMs	Unknown (bring cash just in case)

City	Duncannon
Name of Market	Cove Barn Antique Flea Market
Address	2031 State Road, Duncannon PA 17020
Phone	717-215-5831
Email	N/A
When Market Began	2004 (Building was built in the 1870s!)
Months of Operation	Year-round (But call first in the winter)
Days Open	Sundays and some holidays plus auctions on Fridays at 5 pm
Hours of Operation	Sundays 7 am–4 pm, Fridays 5 pm Auction
Total Size/Acreage	Two floors inside
Number of Outdoor Vendor Spaces	Two acres outside
Space Size	As provided
Tables Provided	No, bring your own
Indoor Buildings and Total Size	Large two-story old barn
Air-Conditioned and/or Heated	Yes
Charge to Vendors	$5 per vendor, first-come first-served
Customer Parking Lot	Vast and free
Food Services	Yes, snack bar
Toilet Facilities	Indoors
ATMs	Maybe, but bring cash

City	**Easton:** See Glendon
City	**East Stroudsburg:** See Marshall's Creek

City	Freeland
Name of Market	Freeland Marketplace
Address	166 Foster Avenue, Freeland, PA 18224
Phone	570-636-1234
Email	N/A
When Market Began	2013
Months of Operation	Year-round, but call first to be sure they are open!
Days Open	Fridays, Saturdays, and Sundays
Hours of Operation	Fridays 12 pm–7pm, Saturdays 9 am–5 pm, Sundays 10 am–4 pm
Total Size/Acreage	Very large!
Number of Outdoor Vendor Spaces	100
Space Size	10' x 10'
Tables Provided	Few, bring your own
Indoor Buildings and Total Size	60,000 sq. ft.
Air-Conditioned and/or Heated	Both
Charge to Vendors	Ranges from $10 to 15 per day, with specials
Customer Parking Lot	250 cars and free
Food Services	Yes, food trucks with ample shaded seating
Toilet Facilities	Two each for men and women and handicap access
ATMs	Yes

City	Glendon (on map, shown as Easton)
Name of Market	Island Park Road Auction and Flea Market
Address	400 Island Park Road, Glendon, PA 18042 (Easton Zip!)
Phone	610-330-9111
Email	N/A
When Market Began	2011
Months of Operation	Year-round
Days Open	*Auctions:* Bi-Monthly (call first); *Indoor Flea Market:* Seven days a week, *Outdoor Flea Market:* Saturdays and Sundays
Hours of Operation	*Indoor Flea Market:* Mon–Fri 10 am– 2 pm, Sat and Sun 8 am– 1 pm; *Outdoor Flea Market:* Sat and Sun 8 am–2 pm or later
Total Size/Acreage	10 acres, in and outdoors
Number of Outdoor Vendor Spaces	40
Space Size	3' x 8'
Tables Provided	Yes
Indoor Buildings and Total Size	Two story, 15,000 sq. ft. (Auctions on second floor)
Air-Conditioned and/or Heated	Yes
Charge to Vendors	Call for details
Customer Parking Lot	100+ cars and free
Food Services	Yes, including beverages
Toilet Facilities	Regular indoor, Porta-Potty outdoor
ATMs	Not sure. Auction House takes credit cards and some checks

City	Kutztown
Name of Market	Renningers Antique & Farm Market
Address	740 Noble Street, Kutztown, PA 19530
Phone	610-683-6848
Email	N/A
When Market Began	50+ Years Ago
Months of Operation	Year-round
Days Open	*Farmer's Market:* Fridays and Saturdays, *Flea Market:* Saturdays
Hours of Operation	Fridays 10 am–7 pm, Saturdays 8 am–4 pm
Total Size/Acreage	40 acres
Number of Outdoor Vendor Spaces	Up to 1,000!
Space Size	Varies
Tables Provided	Yes
Indoor Buildings and Total Size	60,000 sq. ft.
Air-Conditioned and/or Heated	Heated
Charge to Vendors	$5 and up
Customer Parking Lot	Fits hundreds and free
Food Services	Yes! Lots of it
Toilet Facilities	Twenty, indoor and outdoor
ATMs	Yes

City	Marshall's Creek 18335 (Actually E. Stroudsburg 18032)
Name of Market	Pocono Bazaar
Address	1 Municipal Drive/Rt 209, E. Stroudsburg/Marshall's Creek
Phone	570-223-8640
Email	N/A
When Market Began	2012 and many years before nearby
Months of Operation	Year-round
Days Open	Saturdays and Sundays plus holidays, rain or shine
Hours of Operation	9 am–5 pm
Total Size/Acreage	Huge, indoors and outdoors
Number of Outdoor Vendor Spaces	Hundreds, indoors and outdoors
Space Size	Varies
Tables Provided	Yes
Indoor Buildings and Total Size	Massive space
Air-Conditioned and/or Heated	Yes
Charge to Vendors	$25 for used, $50 for new goods, lower by month
Customer Parking Lot	Two big lots and free
Food Services	Yes, food court and food trucks
Toilet Facilities	Yes, nine sets of women's and men's including handicap
ATMs	Yes, and bank on premises too!

City	Mercerberg
Name of Market	Foot Hill Flea Market
Address	6520 Charlestown Road, Mercerberg, PA 17236
Phone	717-360-1275
Email	N/A
When Market Began	2012
Months of Operation	Year-round
Days Open	Saturdays and Sundays
Hours of Operation	9 am–5 pm
Total Size/Acreage	Large building with outside spaces too
Number of Outdoor Vendor Spaces	50+
Space Size	12' x 18'
Tables Provided	Yes
Indoor Buildings and Total Size	Room for 140 vendors indoors
Air-Conditioned and/or Heated	Heated
Charge to Vendors	$10 per day
Customer Parking Lot	Sizeable and free
Food Services	Nice snack bar
Toilet Facilities	Yes
ATMs	No

City	Outskirts of New Hope
Name of Market	Rice's Sale & Country Market
Address	6326 Greenhill Road New Hope, PA 18938
Phone	215-297-5993
Email	N/A
When Market Began	!! 1860 !!
Months of Operation	Year-round on Tuesdays, March through December on Saturday
Days Open	Tuesdays year-round, Saturdays March through December
Hours of Operation	7 am–1 pm and Holidays
Total Size/Acreage	Incredibly huge!
Number of Outdoor Vendor Spaces	400 + some indoors
Space Size	8' x 15' plus room for your vehicle
Tables Provided	Yes. NOTE: paved walkways too, a rarity
Indoor Buildings and Total Size	Several good-sized buildings
Air-Conditioned and/or Heated	Yes
Charge to Vendors	$30 a day, $90 a month new, $20 a day used
Customer Parking Lot	Very large and either free or $1
Food Services	Yes, several options available
Toilet Facilities	Yes, well-attended buildings
ATMs	Yes, three of them

City	Two miles south of New Hope
Name of Market	New Hope Flea Market (Next to Eagle Diner)
Address	6520 Lower York Road(Route 202N), New Hope, PA 18938
Phone	215-862-3111
Email	newhfleamarket@aol.com
When Market Began	1964
Months of Operation	Year-round, but not often in winter
Days Open	Saturdays and Sundays
Hours of Operation	7 am–5 pm
Total Size/Acreage	3 acres
Number of Outdoor Vendor Spaces	50
Space Size	Two six-foot tables
Tables Provided	Yes
Indoor Buildings and Total Size	None
Air-Conditioned and/or Heated	N/A
Charge to Vendors	$10 on Saturdays, $25 on Sundays
Customer Parking Lot	Ample and free
Food Services	In Eagle Diner alongside market
Toilet Facilities	Same as above
ATMs	Same as above

City	Quakertown
Name of Market	Quakertown Farmer's & Flea Market
Address	201 Station Road Quakertown, PA 18951
Phone	215-536-4115
Email	N/A
When Market Began	1932
Months of Operation	Year-round
Days Open	Fridays, Saturdays, and Sundays
Hours of Operation	Fridays and Saturdays 9am–9 pm, Sundays 10 am–5 pm
Total Size/Acreage	30 acres
Number of Outdoor Vendor Spaces	100
Space Size	3' x 8' plus room for vehicle
Tables Provided	Yes
Indoor Buildings and Total Size	Yes, plus outdoor barn
Air-Conditioned and/or Heated	Both
Charge to Vendors	Varies, as low as $50 for all three days
Customer Parking Lot	Large and free
Food Services	Yes, indoors and outdoors
Toilet services	Ample indoor toilets
ATMs	Yes, two of them

City	Sinking Spring
Name of Market	Willow Glen Flea Market
Address	94 Park Avenue, Sinking Spring, PA 19608
Phone	610-777-6388
Email	heather@konopelski.com
When Market Began	Early 1990s
Months of Operation	April through November
Days Open	Sundays only
Hours of Operation	5 am–1 pm
Total Size/Acreage	More than two acres
Number of Outdoor Vendor Spaces	Up to 200
Space Size	20' x 20'
Tables Provided	No, bring your own
Indoor Buildings and Total Size	None
Air-Conditioned and/or Heated	N/A
Charge to Vendors	$14 a day
Customer Parking Lot	Holds up to 500 cars and free
Food Services	Yes, catered on premises.
Toilet Facilities	Yes, two separate buildings for men and women
ATMs	Yes

New Jersey

City	Berlin
Name of Market	Berlin Farmer's Market
Address	41 Clementon Road, Berlin, NJ 08009
Phone	856-767-1246
Email	bfmmkt@eticomm.net
When Market Began	1940
Months of Operation	Year-round, but subject to weather outside
Days Open	*Indoor:* Thursdays through Sundays, *Flea Market:* Saturdays and Sundays
Hours of Operation	*Indoor:* Thurs to Sat 10 am–9 pm, Sun 10 am–6 pm; *Flea Market:* Sat and Sun 8 am to 4 pm
Total Size/Acreage	Quite large
Number of Outdoor Vendor Spaces	700+!
Space Size	12' x 30' and variable too
Tables Provided	Yes, but first-come first-served for them
Indoor Buildings and Total Size	Large, room for 70+ vendors
Air-Conditioned and/or Heated	Yes
Charge to Vendors	$30 one day, $35 two days, and up
Customer Parking Lot	Large and free
Food Services	Yes
Toilet Facilities	Two each inside and Porta-Potties outside
ATMs	Yes
NOTE: this market has quite a few logical rules, especially about used vs. new items.	

City	Columbus
Name of Market	Columbus Farmer's Market
Address	2919 Route 206, Columbus, NJ 08022
Phone	609-267-0400
Email	N/A
When Market Began	1929
Months of Operation	Year-round
Days Open	Thursdays, Saturdays, and Sundays
Hours of Operation	From 6:00 am until much later
Total Size/Acreage	200+ acres!
Number of Outdoor Vendor Spaces	Up to 2,100!
Space Size	12' x 30', including your vehicle
Tables Provided	Yes
Indoor Buildings and Total Size	Sizeable, holds 65+ different vendors
Air-Conditioned and/or Heated	Yes
Charge to Vendors	Varies from $20 used, $30 new products and up
Customer Parking Lot	Huge areas and free
Food Services	Yes, quite a variety too
Toilet Facilities	Four indoor men's and women's and 22 Porta-Potties
ATMs	Yes, four of them

City	Dover
Name	Dover Flea Market
Address	18 W. Blackwell Street, Dover, NJ 07801
Phone	973-389-7870
Email	doverfleamarket@aol.com
When Market Began	1998
Months of Operation	From Easter Sunday through Thanksgiving
Days Open	Sundays
Hours of Operation	9 am–4 pm
Total Size/Acreage	3 acres +
Number of Outdoor Vendor Spaces	100
Space Size	25' x 10'
Tables Provided	No, bring your own
Indoor Buildings and Total Size	None
Air-Conditioned and/or Heated	N/A
Charge to Vendors	$40 to $75
Customer Parking Lot	Can hold up to 750 vehicles and free
Food Services	Food vendors on premises
Toilet Facilities	Seven Porta-Potties, including handicapped
ATMs	No

City	East Rutherford (at the Meadowlands)
Name of Market	New Meadowlands Flea Market
Address	50 Route 120, East Rutherford, NJ 07030
Phone	973-789-1106
Email	vendorsamerica@aol.com
When Market Began	1991
Months of Operation	Year-round
Days Open	Saturdays
Hours of Operation	8 am–4 pm
Total Size/Acreage	Three large lots
Number of Outdoor Vendor Spaces	500
Space Size	25' x 18' or larger
Tables Provided	No, bring your own tables
Indoor Buildings and Total Size	None
Air-Conditioned and/or Heated	N/A
Charge to Vendors	$100 a day or more
Customer Parking Lot	Huge, room for several thousand
Food Services	Yes, yearly contracted vendors
Toilet Facilities	Yes, a trailer plus dozens of attended Porta-Potties
ATMs	Yes

City	Englishtown
Name of Market	Englishtown Auction
Address	90 Wilson Avenue, Englishtown, NJ 07726
Phone	732-446-9644
Email	N/A
When Market Began	1929
Months of Operation	Year-round
Days Open	Saturdays and Sundays, plus holidays
Hours of Operation	8 am–4 pm rain or shine
Total Size/Acreage	40 acres outside plus five buildings
Number of Outdoor Vendor Spaces	Hundreds
Space Size	Varies
Tables Provided	Yes
Indoor Buildings and Total Size	Five
Air-Conditioned and/or Heated	Maybe
Charge to Vendors	Varies from as little as $5 daily per month
Customer Parking Lot	Very large and free
Food Services	Yes, quite a variety too
Toilet Facilities	Yes
ATMs	Probably, but bring cash just in case

City	Lambertville (two miles south)
Name of Market	Golden Nugget Antiques Flea Market
Address	1850 River Road/Route 29, Lambertville, NJ 08530
Phone	609-397-0811
Email	N/A
When Market Began	1967
Months of Operation	Year-round
Days Open	Wednesdays, Saturdays, and Sundays, plus holidays
Hours of Operation	6 am–4 pm
Total Size/Acreage	Huge!
Number of Outdoor Vendor Spaces	Nearly 400!
Space Size	About 10' x 15' plus room for vehicle behind your space
Tables Provided	Yes
Indoor Buildings and Total Size	Several
Air-Conditioned and/or Heated	Yes
Charge to Vendors	$25 a space or less outdoors
Customer Parking Lot	Quite ample and free
Food Services	Yes, in café on premises
Toilet Facilities	Yes, Porta-Potties
ATMs	Yes, but bring cash anyway

City	Neshanic Station (Somerset County)
Name of Market	Neshanic Flea Market
Address	100 Elm Street, Neshanic Station, NJ 08853
Phone	908-369-3660
Email	N/A
When Market Began	Lots of years ago!
Months of Operation	March through December
Days Open	Sundays, weather permitting
Hours of Operation	8 am until everyone goes home
Total Size/Acreage	Several acres
Number of Outdoor Vendor Spaces	About 60
Space Size	Enough for your table and vehicle
Tables Provided	No, bring your own
Indoor Buildings and Total Size	No (*)
Air-Conditioned and/or Heated	N/A
Charge to Vendors	$10 a day
Customer Parking Lot	Sufficient and free
Food Services	(*) Yes, diner on premises run by owner
Toilet Facilities	(*) Yes, inside diner
ATMs	No

City	Palmyra
Name of Market	Tacony-Palmyra Flea Market
Address	201 Route 73 South, Palmyra, NJ 08065
Phone	856-829-3000
Email	N/A
When Market Began	1980 or so
Months of Operation	Year-round
Days Open	Saturdays and Sundays and some holidays
Hours of Operation	6 am–3 pm
Total Size/Acreage	Very large
Number of Outdoor Vendor Spaces	430
Space Size	18' x 18'
Tables Provided	No, bring your own
Indoor Buildings and Total Size	No
Air-Conditioned and/or Heated	N/A
Charge to Vendors	$75 reserved space, or $55 for others
Customer Parking Lot	Two large lots and free
Food Services	Yes, food stand on premises, run by manager
Toilet Facilities	Yes, lots of them and all indoors
ATMs	No

City	Paterson and elsewhere in Passaic County PLUS one in Bergen*
Name of Market	Jar Promotions; St. Gerards Flea Market and elsewhere
Address	501 W. Broadway, Paterson, NJ 07522* and other locations
*This one-of-a-kind market travels from one scheduled site to another, and according to Jar, all profit from vendors' fees are given to charities like churches, Boy Scouts, etc.	
Phone	973-389-8357, 973-981-00049
Email	jarpro673@aol.com
When Market Began	1987
Months of Operation	Year-round
Days Open	First and Third Sunday; Second and Fourth Saturday each month
Hours of Operation	7 am–4:30 pm
Total Size/Acreage	Sizeable and varies
Number of Outdoor Vendor Spaces	20–60
Space Size	Two parking lot spaces per vendor
Tables Provided	No, bring your own
Indoor Buildings and Total Size	None
The sites are outdoors only, and the operator takes the market to 8 to 10 different locations every month, mostly in Passaic County.	
Air-Conditioned and/or Heated	N/A
Charge to Vendors	As low as $30 per month
Customer Parking Lot	Ample and free
Food Services	No
Toilet Facilities	Yes, in buildings on premises
ATMs	No

City	White Township (Belvidere Zip Code, 07823)
Name of Market	White Township Flea Market
Address	421 US 46 East, Belvidere, NJ 07823 (in White Township)
Phone	908-303-1608
Email	N/A
When Market Began	1960s
Months of Operation	Year-round
Days Open	Saturdays and Sundays
Hours of Operation	7 am–4 pm
Total Size/Acreage	5 acres+
Number of Outdoor Vendor Spaces	75
Space Size	10' x 25'
Tables Provided	No, bring your own
Indoor Buildings and Total Size	One 2,000 sq. ft. building
Air-Conditioned and/or Heated	No
Charge to Vendors	$20 each Saturday, $25 each Sunday
Customer Parking Lot	Room for 100+ vehicles
Food Services	Yes, food truck
Toilet Facilities	Yes, two for men and two for women
ATMs	Across the street at Quik-Check

Insurance

Chances are pretty good that at least 75% of all merchants who are selling goods not only don't carry any insurance but also may not even know what kinds of protection to buy. This chapter will describe what insurance might be needed and how to buy it. (I was a business insurance expert for 40+ years).

First of all, I retired way back at the end of 1994 so much of my knowledge is as old as the guy writing these words. So to be sure I was bringing you dear readers the up-to-date data, I turned to Morgan McLachlan, the guy who my former partner and I merged our business with back then to get current information. As an aside, if you have any insurance questions you can reach Morgan at 908-526-4600, or at morgan@ insuranceagent.com.

Most vendors own a home or rent an apartment and 99% of you carry some form of homeowners insurance, right? Well, even though the contents of your mansion are covered with insurance, the stuff you bring to flea markets to sell is not covered by insurance, because every Homeowners policy contains an exclusion for "business property." Some policies can be changed to include business pursuits if you are a professional; a doctor, accountant, etc., running your practice out of your home but a flea market vendor? Not so much!

So to deal with this you either need to buy a specific policy or at least realize that you may be running bare without protection. The standard policy usually purchased is called a "BOP," or a Business Owners Policy. This policy covers your property against fire, etc., at your premises as well as while elsewhere. If you buy, for example, a policy limit of $10,000 covering your stock for sale, as well as your office contents, i.e. desk, computer, etc., then the "BOP" will give you a 10% limit of coverage elsewhere, as in at a flea market and while en route to and from the market. Oh yeah, note that I talked here about your computer, etc. Here too, if it, your desk, etc., were purchased out of a business checking account that you run your flea enterprise through, that stuff too is not protected against loss or damage under your homeowners policy.

It's always tricky trying to figure out what your claim dollar total may be because determining the "value" of the destroyed property is not clear. Generally they go based on "wholesale" value of the merchandise and the office goods are valued differently too.

One more thing, hopes are that you will make a buck doing this right? Well, if you carry a "BOP," your loss of income will also be covered therein. Determining what income you might have lost is tricky but at least, you have a chance this way.

Got a headache yet? I've only begun to start. The larger flea markets may require you to buy liability insurance, covering you and maybe even them, against a law suit brought by someone who gets injured at your table or while using the things they bought from you. "Product Liability" is usually included within the "BOP" as is coverage against the direct injury caused at your table. Besides product liability, every "BOP" protects you against other liability claims like a person being injured at your table in the same manner as your next-door neighbor may get hurt in your home — covered by your Homeowners policy.

Let's assume that you get really fancy and operate a triple table and you hire a guy to help sell your goods. Folks, under the table or off the books, whatever you want to call it, if he gets hurt and you hadn't purchased "Worker's Compensation" insurance, woe is you. A court could award the injured person X dollars and if they find out you were uninsured, they could double that award!

All right, you are a big success, and expand to run booths at two or more markets at the same time, hiring a friend or two to run the other ones. Guess what? You may also need an "Employee Dishonesty Bond," honest, to cover what they may steal from you!

Legal Sales vs. Not-So-Legal Sales

T ricky, some merchants have no idea what they may not be allowed to sell, so I will try to explain the nuances of this matter herein. Discussed a bit earlier, let's talk about this again and in further detail. Starting with ...

Outside Food: I talked to folks at the Health office of counties in both New Jersey and Pennsylvania and the consensus of opinion ran pretty much the same way. You cannot sell food outside of buildings; that is food that is not tightly pre-packaged, unless you have a license to do so. You are not supposed to handle the food for sure. I was at a market one day where two guys were selling dozens and dozens of wonderfully tasty rolls and breads. They used a great gimmick to aide in their sales but it may not have been 100% exactly in line with the law though.

They would reach into a cooler and take out a cheese, cut a piece off and place it on a slice of bread and top the whole deal off with a bit of sun-dried tomato. From the looks of those sampling the goods, this stuff was to die for. However, while the merchants really tried by wearing rubber gloves and such, they also handled the cash that customers were handing them for whole loaves. The tasty samples caused a huge load of people to buy the breads and this really was a neat idea, but, hey, maybe not according to "code." Merchants who sell food at markets indoor or out, also must have a facility food license.

In Burlington County, my New Jersey source referred me to N.J.A.C. 8:24, Chapter 24, the sanitary code but maybe your best idea as a merchant is to consult someone in your town to check it all out. My contact in Bucks County, Pennsylvania was of a similar view.

The key is cleanliness and selling food from indoors doesn't guaranty anything, however, it stands to reason that it may be a little easier to pick up germs outdoors, right?

Dead Stuff: Here again, I was concerned about what can be sold outdoors at our markets so I asked someone who should know, one of the fine representatives of the New Jersey Fish & Wildlife Commission, a woman in law enforcement. And I'm fairly sure that a similar rule applies in Pennsylvania too. The N.J. Game Code can be found at N.J.S.A. 23 and my concern was about things you actually do find at some markets, usually quite innocently being displayed.

For example: How about stuffed fish, or maybe mounted birds, ditto deer heads, and add to that "skins?" The bottom line is that most of these things cannot be sold at a market unless the item being offered passes muster by being in compliance with the law that permits someone to have actually killed the critter. So if you are selling a beautiful and brightly colored cock turkey; you may need to have an up-to-date hunting license with you and maybe, in some instances as with a deer, the appropriate tag too.

I was at a market and fellow vendors were talking about snake skins as well as fur pelts and I wondered out loud if any law forbade such displays and my F&G source said that for sure, you had better check the law because you may be in violation.

What to Wear,
Vendors and Shoppers

Few outdoor markets are open all winter long but some are, especially those containing buildings from which vendors may sell their goods with protection from cold and wind, as well as from extreme heat.

Umbrellas: Not wearing appropriate clothing can destroy an otherwise pleasant day. Start off on a normal day with nice weather expected and be you a merchant or buyer, always have an umbrella with you just in case — that's warning number one.

Hand-Warmers: Go to a sporting goods store before hitting the market and buy yourself a few of those handy-dandy little chemically treated hand warmers if the day is expected to be cold. I never go fishing in chilly weather without having some with me and they have often saved the day for me. When walking around a market for an hour or two, the last thing you want is to be cold. Let's take this point down the trail a bit more. Wear a shirt or jacket that has two chest pockets! And no, I'm not nuts. Take the package, open it up, shake it if needed to kick the warming agent into gear; and then place one package into each pocket and feel the warmth. And no, you don't have to write me and say thanks, a silent acknowledgment is all you must do, I may even feel your thanks.

Merchants need these hand-warmers, like they used to say, "in spades." Six hours in the outdoors are the rule, more or less, and if you don't have what I call "booby-warmers" in place, and it is chilly outside, you may never return to a flea market table again as a seller.

Let's talk further about this, vendors — You may even want to go on line and find a source where you can buy a carton or two of these wonderful packets in bulk for sale to your customers or to fellow vendors. Everyone who buys these from you will never forget it and will always remember to say thanks the next time they pass your table.

They generally sell for a buck or two per two-baggie package and normally provide heat for eight to ten hours. You may need to wrap them in a tissue or handkerchief because they might even be too warm for you! While I have never used any, they also come in smaller packages for insertion into your boots.

Please wash your hands before eating because you may need to cleanse them of any chemicals that rub off the pack.

Layers: Sorry to tell you what 99% of you already knew, because if you go to sporting events, all of you know to dress in layers so that you can take off or add as needed. But if you are a sheltered indoor type, make sure you bring an extra layer or two with you. A scarf is a neat addition as well, ditto a stocking/"watch" cap. Gloves, for sure, as well. Forget the ear muffs because someone will start to mock you at this point.

Foot Coverings: Again, maybe silly to bother writing about, but there may be a few folks who go somewhere without proper shoes being worn. I actually saw a guy walking around with, I kid you not, Dutch wooden shoes at one market, honest. I think they used to be called "Klompens" when I was in school but by any other spelling, close your eyes and picture how incredibly uncomfortable he was. Hey, maybe it was a fraternity deal?

But wooden shoes to the side, wear something soft and comfortable. You will be walking around for an hour or two as a shopper and vendors need this even more. You may be on your feet and/or seated for six or more hours. So forget hard shoes and leave the sandals or slippers home. A nice pair of sneakers is best of all. Most markets, no nearly all markets, have aisles that are paved with stone, hard sand, and sometimes mush. So foot comfort is critical. Open-toed sandals may be good for the beach but stumble into a stone or worse, a piece of glass and you will realize why I am begging you to not wear them.

Cover Your Head! Again, sorry to say the obvious, but, especially baldies like me, all must wear something that covers their heads, protecting against sunburn. I don't care if you wear SPF 99; sun burning down on the top of your head sure isn't the best way to deal with skin cancer!

White Socks! Never thought of this one, did you, even my fellow vendors? It came to me once while sitting at my table in the beautiful warmth of the day. Wearing black socks, by 10:30 or so, the sun had raised highly enough to really warm my face and bring expectations of a great day of selling ahead. After all, most markets do their best business between 10 and 11 am or so and the best of the day lie ahead. However, it got warmer, and my feet got too warm, and I went from very comfortable to quite uncomfortable quickly. So the message here is to wear white socks and I betcha never thought of this one, huh?

Vendor at the New Hope Flea Market.

How to Make Your Booth/Products Stand Out

E very market provides either space or actual tables to their vendors. But what a vendor does with their space is another subject and the way they present their goods can produce far more sales if done well.

A Tent: The top "plus" would apply if a vendor can protect their space with a portable pop-up tent. Of course the tent must fit well into your space and not overlap it because that wouldn't be fair to your neighbor vendors.

The tent has to be sturdy though because a strong wind could literally lift it off the ground causing injury (see Insurance in Chapter 13!) Pick a color of your choice but if cheap enough, find something bright and light so that it may appeal to shoppers. Be sure that it has plenty of room on which to place hangers if you are trying to sell clothing and the like because this will increase your selling space. Again, don't block your neighbor from the view of passersby. That's not nice and it's been done to me and it got me cranky.

Besides offering more area to display merchandise, a tent offers cover! If it rains, hey, stay under the tent and keep dry. Better yet, it will keep your merchandise dry too. And if it really starts to pour, watch how much interest in your stock takes place. People come on in and shop or at least try to make it look like they are shopping and whether it is based on guilt or maybe even your stuff really attracts their attention because they became a captive audience, your tent could double your sales!

Tablecloths: Clearly, if you are at the typical market which provides big, old tables, you really don't want to try and encourage customers to stop and visit if they can see some of the tables I've seen. So find out how large your table is and bring a brightly colored cloth with you. It may make your products really stand out too.

Stones: Yeah, stones, wanna make something out of it? If you are selling, among other items, clothing, T-shirts and the like, maybe old post cards and for that matter, anything that the wind can lift up and carry away, bring some stones with you. Stick them under your table, just in case it blows, and use them as required. You'll thank me for this one!

Lift Your Merchandise: Especially if you are selling costume jewelry, build a small appliance onto which you can place your goods so that it will be easier to see your wares. In the case of jewelry, cover your display lift with a velvet-like surface in black or maybe deep blue or green, whatever color fits your fancy and makes you think it will draw attention. This really works very well when it is sunny outside. The sparkle of what could actually be cheap costume jewelry, lifted up into the sunlight can really jack up your sales, big time. It may be subliminal, but it works every time.

Smile! You rarely get a shot at a buyer more than once a show so if you are in the car, grabbing a smoke or maybe a snack, or even taking a toilet break, visiting with a neighbor, etc., and a customer passes by without looking at your table, that's one more loss of a potential sale. So be there as much of the day as you can and stick a smile on your kisser and use it! Put a smile in your mouth and release it with a nice greeting, if only a pleasant, "Hi!" Many buyers are intimidated by such greetings and look away but those are the folks who are only at the market under severe distress, obliged to attend by their housemate under extreme threat of a serious penalty being enforced.

A smiley "Hi!" could bring that person over to your table and create some sales and even if only gets a pleasant "HI!" back, that isn't all bad either, right?

Stickers/Tags: We very briefly talked about "tag sales" earlier but in this part, let's discuss just how important a tag may really be to you. And if not a tag, then a little sticker/label. Some buyers really don't like surprises and also don't want to ask the vendor how much they want for an item of interest. So carry a supply of little stringed tags as well as stickers onto which you can place the asking price for your goods. You can always offer a discount or accept a lower offer but at least, in this manner, you have prepared your buyer with a strategy to work with. Always have a few pens, which you can use to write on the tags or stickers and try to be certain that they aren't runny ink pens!

Signs: Make up a few signs at home that mark things that should appeal to your buyers. Things like price, for sure. Maybe something which says "two for one," or buy one, get another of equal or lesser value at half-price, etc.? Try to use indelible ink for the signs and without doubt, bring a roll or two of Scotch Tape to help keep the signs in place. And you can really make a good friend if a neighbor needs some tape and you give him a few strips.

Toilet Paper: Yeah! Toilet paper. I have yet to go into a "facility" at any flea market I've attended that was without TP, but just in case, bring a roll. Here too, your neighbor may really love you for it.

Plastic Display Holders: Depending on what you are selling, if it can fit in or stand up on a plastic display rack, kind of like what I use to make my books more appealing to shoppers, by all means, buy some. Go on line if need be to find them but they really are quite useful and may even take up less space than if you lie the stock flat on the table. Stick it up in their eyes with these holders and you will probably increase your sales this way.

Acquiring Stock!

I t may have been a better idea for me to start here rather than end at this point because vendors who are clueless regarding how to gather things to sell start off with a major handicap. Sure, your mom's attic junk, ditto what is in your basement or garage that you don't want are a few normal places but let's separate you from the regular folks and bring some more ideas to the table.

You've already read some thoughts from my contributors but let me expand and add to what they suggested.

Dead People Stuff: Yes, gruesome but still if you have customers that like antiques, what better place to find old things than in the attic or basement of a dead guy. Not just relatives in fact, but strangers too. Estate Sales are always held when the occupants of homes have passed on. So when you read about an Estate Sale, get to it and check out what your competition is. You may find that the place is nearly empty. Some of these are run as auctions but others are simply a spot where someone is trying to offload a house full of unwanted items.

Bring a pile of cash with you to these events and you could fill up your pickup truck with loads of quite saleable stock at extremely low price to you.

Obituary Notices: Okay, still more gruesome an idea is to read the obituary notices in your local newspaper. If you see an unusual name and an old age for the deceased, you may be able to go on line and do a look-up for an address. Most such notices tell you what town the deceased had lived in. They don't give actual addresses any longer for good reason. But if an eighty-year-old person with a four-syllable name died and they listed the town of residence, chances are fairly good that you can look up their actual address by simply seeking their telephone number, again, via Google. Try it four or five times and my guess is that you will find the actual address at least one time and then go to the house and see if anyone is home. If a child or other relative of the deceased is there, you could get hollered at, big time, but some people may actually be relieved that someone is at the door to take unwanted material away. Try it, okay?

Garbage Day: Not just your own neighborhood either. Call your own garbage contractor and ask them to tell you what other days they pick up trash and at what nearby streets. And then, the night before, simply drive around and "shop." I've often seen some really good "trash" sitting out there for the taking, and much of this is kids' toys in good condition, merely outgrown.

If this "gathering" style works, expand it to other nearby towns. You could acquire more stock, good stuff too, than you could dream of and the best part of it is that it is FREE! It isn't a good idea to open the trash cans though, this is probably illegal and for sure, it may bring you a visit from a furry occupant of the garbage can — yikes!

Pay for It: (But not too much). Buying stock is the easiest way to fill your table but laying out money is never fun. Getting it free is sure the best way, right? But you can still buy a load of material at very low price if done correctly. Go to the neighborhood combined garage sales. Find them listed in your local newspaper and the free newspapers are best of all for this information. You could find a dozen or more homeowners out there competing for your cash and cutting their prices deep to the bone in order to get your money.

The same idea applies to other markets like religious or charitable ones. Getting money is their goal and not money for their own pockets. This could cause the person running the sale to cut prices way, way down low. Show up early and scope things out. You may even be able to buy before opening time if a seller is on premises. Many will advertise

"NOT BEFORE 9 am," or such, but you aren't breaking any law by looking, right?

If you are patient, you may even want to wait until the selling time is nearing its end. If half the material remains, this is when to pounce with a foolishly low (to you) offer. The last things these sellers want is to find a way to get the material back to whoever brought it so a low-ball offer is often a wonderful way to buy and even to sell.

On-Line Shopping: eBay and Craigslist come to mind as two on-line stores that folks use to buy items at low cost. And I'm not just talking about single item purchases either. You can acquire stock in bulk at low cost in this manner. Check it out. Most large sellers allow you to buy via PayPal, credit card, etc. and, for example, I found wholesalers who sell costume jewelry of every style and price imaginable while doing this research. And you don't only have to seek merchandise being offered either. You can simply type in what you are looking for and you will probably be shocked to see what responses you will get.

Other Flea Markets: Find the smaller markets and you could find lots of things being offered for sale with more sellers than buyers in attendance. When you locate an empty market, with few if any shoppers, this is the time to get selfish and start shopping to fill your wagon. Prices drop drastically at poorly attended markets, especially as closing time nears. Don't get obnoxious with your offers but realize that you have taken over the driver's seat.

The same idea applies to every other market around. Low-ball offers are at least ones that may get the seller to obtain some money for what they otherwise will go home with. Clearly, if it is produce, fresh produce, buy it cheap and attend a market the next day and sell it as one-day old corn, tomatoes, etc. And sell it you will, at nice profit.

Epilogue

Lots of readers turn to the back of a book before even looking at its table of contents in order to determine whether or not they may want to buy the book. This section belongs to you backward readers. The market for this book is limitless, including most folks who buy and sell things, period! Just turn to your fellow workers and chances are good that at least half of them have been to one flea market or another and might really benefit from reading our book.

This book should appeal to all types of not-for-profit organizations who do fund-raising to help grow their bank balances. Out-of-work people may benefit by getting the kind of knowledge needed to start to sell products at flea markets. Stores that are going out of business would clearly love to find a place that they can offload unsold inventory at. Bargain hunters too should love this book because of the ideas that they gather from it.

From personal knowledge, I can attest to the fact that all walks of life are represented at the flea markets that I have attended. Race, religion, etc., are not a factor at all because just looking at those selling and buying, you can easily see that nothing matters. T-shirts carry the names of a dozen or more colleges at every market. Baseball caps, derbies, wooden shoes, top hats, all are seen on sellers and buyers alike.

So the message is "BUY THIS BOOK!" You just may really enjoy reading and learning from it!

Manny

Dog in costume parade at Rice's.

DONE READING?
MAYBE NOT!

WANT TO BUY HUGE VOLUMES OF MERCHANDISE AT LOW PRICES?

Dear readers, I just found something that needs to be added in for sellers:

As you went through this book, you found lots of ideas about how to gather merchandise for sale. But while at a flea market in Lake Worth, Florida, of all places, I was handed a copy of the November, 2014 edition of *East Coast Merchandiser*, a fine publication.

Among other items I found for sale in the magazine, in no particular order, were various items of fashion in minimum orders of a pallet; baseball caps, by the dozen; playing cards with a minimum order of $150; slippers and boots, by the case, etc. Bottom line? You have to order in quantity but the prices are very low!

This magazine is available by buying a subscription but most of the 100,000 copies they distribute monthly are given out free of charge at hundreds of markets across the country.

The publisher, Jeff Dwight, told me that they began back in the late 1980s and that they focus on telling prospective vendors how to obtain stock at inexpensive prices and the way they do that is by selling advertisements to wholesalers. Prospective sellers can get a copy of the magazine at modest cost by sending an e-mail to circulation manager, Lisa

Evans, at lisae@sumnercom.com. If that doesn't work, then call East
Coast Merchandiser at 800-999-8281, ext. 127, and ask that they mail a
copy to you for payment. It really would be worth the call!

So if you want to get lots of inexpensive merchandise to offer to your
customers, please add this idea to your shopping list! And check their
web site out at fleamarketzone.com.

Order Form

For additional copies of this book or any of my other books, please fill out this form and send check or money order to:

Gone Fishin' Enterprises
PO Box 556, Annandale, NJ 08801

- New Jersey residents please add 7% sales tax.
- If you'd like the book autographed, please tell me what name to use.
- Shipping is free!

For bulk orders call: 908-996-2145
You can also order on the web at **www.gonefishinbooks.com**.

- -

Name _____

Address _____

City _____ State _____ Zip _____

Autograph to _____

Copies	Book	Price
_____	Gone Fishin'... For Beginners	$13.95
_____	Gone Fishin'... With Kids	$9.99
_____	Sport Fish of New Jersey: An Angler's Guide	$16.95
_____	Gone Fishin': The 100 Best Spots in New Jersey	$16.95
_____	Gone Fishin': The 100 Best Spots in New York	$16.95
_____	Gone Fishin'... Florida's 100 Best Salt Waters	$13.95
_____	Gone Fishin': The 75 Best Waters in Connecticut	$13.95
_____	Gone Fishin': Massachusetts' 100 Best Waters	$14.95
_____	Gone Fishin': The 50 Best Waters in Pennsylvania	$13.95
_____	Gone Fishin'... For Hybrid Bass	$13.95
_____	Gone Fishin'... In Round Valley Reservoir	$13.95
_____	Gone Fishin'... In Spruce Run Reservoir	$12.95
_____	Gone Fishin'... In N.J. Saltwater Rivers and Bays	$14.95
_____	Gone Fishin'... For Carp	$12.95
_____	Gone Fishin'... In Lake Hopatcong	$13.95
_____	So You Want to Write a Book	$13.95
_____	How to Sell a Condo or Townhouse (or Rent One Out)	$14.95
_____	The Flea Market Book for Vendors and Shoppers	$9.99